The Gauchos
ARGENTINA

Rob Waring, *Series Editor*

NATIONAL GEOGRAPHIC
LEARNING

Australia • Brazil • Mexico • Singapore • United Kingdom • United States

Words to Know

This story is set in three different areas of Argentina: Corrientes [kɔriɛnteɪz], Patagonia [pætəgoʊniə], and Salta.

 Argentinean Gauchos. Read the paragraph. Then match each word with the correct definition.

Argentina has many different types of terrain, including the wet, flat *pampas* of Corrientes, the windy plains of Patagonia, and the hills of Salta. In remote areas of the country, far away from busy city life, one can find traditional Argentinean gauchos. These gauchos love their self-reliant lifestyle and enjoy living on their own. They are also very proud of their heritage and want to keep their traditions alive for future generations.

1. terrain _____

2. *pampas* _____

3. remote _____

4. gaucho _____

5. self-reliant _____

6. heritage _____

a. a Spanish word for the plains in parts of South America

b. far away from cities and towns

c. able to take care of oneself without outside help

d. the natural features of land; the landscape

e. the cultural traditions, beliefs, and history of a specific group

f. a South American person who cares for large farm animals as a job

B The Life of a Gaucho. Read the paragraph. Then write the number of the correct <u>underlined</u> word next to each item in the picture.

1. <u>Cattle</u> are groups of large animals raised for milk, food, and leather.
2. <u>Chaps</u> are leather coverings worn over a gaucho's pants.
3. A <u>poncho</u> is a piece of clothing shaped like a blanket with a hole for one's head.
4. A <u>ranch</u> is a very large farm which usually raises animals.
5. A <u>saddle</u> is the leather seat used for riding animals, usually horses.
6. <u>Reins</u> are long pieces of leather connected to an animal's head or mouth and used to control it.

A Gaucho from Salta on a Ranch

In the country of Argentina, cowboy life has scarcely changed over the past three centuries. For most people, the gaucho is a hero here; he is a legendary figure that is larger than life. But in the far reaches of the country, there are still men for whom the gaucho story is more than a legend. For them, it is their life; they are the real gauchos of Argentina.

The cowboy life of the gaucho came to Argentina from the Spanish culture. It created a unique type of men who were as hardy and self-reliant as the animals for which they cared. The word 'gaucho' is a South American Indian word which means 'outcast,' or one who doesn't belong to a specific society or group. These tough men were given the name because they lived outside of the limits of society and they desired freedom and independence. There are as many kinds of gauchos as there are varied terrains in Argentina, which include: the soft flat *pampas* of Corrientes, the windswept plains of Patagonia, and the wooded hills of Salta. Each of these regions has its own distinct type of gaucho.

 CD 2, Track 03

In a remote region of Corrientes, located in the northeast of Argentina, lives **Don José Ansola**.[1] Don José is a 76-year-old horseman who seems to be the 'classic gaucho'; a man who is typical of gauchos all over this large country. Don José treasures the remoteness of his residence. He believes that **solitude**[2] helps to keep gaucho life in its purest form, and the remote location of his estate helps him to maintain it.

Don José describes how the countryside is part of the gaucho lifestyle, and how much he loves living there. "If I couldn't live in the *campo*, [or] the countryside—an unthinkable thought—I don't know what I'd do," he explains. He says that he would rather live in a poor little house in the country than in a palace in the city. He also states that if he lived in the city, he would miss too many things from country life. He would miss the sound of the horses running, the call of the birds at dawn, and drinking traditional Argentinean *mate*[3] in the clean country air.

---

[1] **Don José Ansola:** [dɒn hoʊseɪ ænsoʊlə]
[2] **solitude:** the state of being alone for long periods of time
[3] *mate:* a traditional type of South American tea

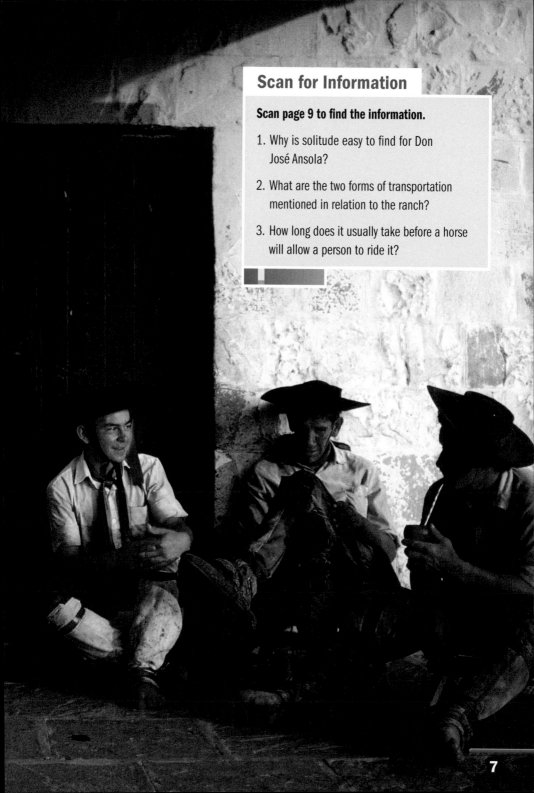

Scan for Information

Scan page 9 to find the information.

1. Why is solitude easy to find for Don José Ansola?

2. What are the two forms of transportation mentioned in relation to the ranch?

3. How long does it usually take before a horse will allow a person to ride it?

Don José's 400-square-kilometer* ranch in Corrientes is far away from everything. There are no roads in or out, which means that visitors are rare. Airplanes are the only way of getting to and from the ranch. On the ranch itself, Don José depends entirely on his horses to travel around—they constitute an absolutely essential part of the lifestyle at his home. As a result, Don José and his three sons spend much of their time finding and catching the wild horses that run free in the countryside. The gauchos require several horses in order to operate their ranch, but first, the horses must be 'broken' so that they will allow people to ride on their backs.

Don José explains that it takes a considerable amount of time to break a horse so that a man can ride it. "Breaking a horse is a slow process, taking more than a year," he reports, and it's not particularly easy. While they are being broken, the horses are sometimes treated quite roughly and occasionally end up kicking, jumping, or rolling on the ground. "This is something the horse learns to **put up with**,"[4] explains Don José. The gaucho then adds that the horse must adjust to being ridden so that the riders aren't injured or thrown off the animal later. The treatment makes one wonder whether or not it is cruel to break horses in this way, but according to Don José it's actually not. The training, Don José says, often seems **harsher**[5] than it really is. In fact, a close bond exists between horse and gaucho. "We love our horses, and in the end, they love us in return," says Don José. He then continues with pride, "This is the traditional way of training a horse in Argentina—the gaucho way."

---

* see page 32 for a metric conversion chart

[4] **put up with:** accept treatment that is unpleasant over a period of time

[5] **harsh:** very difficult; strict

Being a gaucho is more than leading a life of solitude and caring for horses and cattle. The gaucho way of life also has its own strict code of **ethics**.[6] **Hospitality**[7] and respect for others are as much a part of this lifestyle as the art of breaking horses. Unfortunately, Argentina is nearly the last place in the world where the gaucho code is still maintained and the demanding lifestyle still exists. It is home to nearly 150,000 gauchos, who are very much a part of the national identity. One reason for their popularity is that gauchos are a universal part of Argentinean life. There are gauchos living in all parts of the country, even 2,000 kilometers south of Buenos Aires, on the edge of Antarctica in a place called Patagonia.

[6] **ethics:** correct behavior
[7] **hospitality:** friendly treatment of others, especially in offering food, drink, and a comfortable place to be

Patagonia is a very remote and strange-looking land. The Andes mountain range, with its huge ancient **glaciers**,[8] contributes to the uniqueness of the landscape. The region looks as if it comes from another world; freezing, cold and empty, except for some very **exotic**[9] animals.

This harsh Patagonian terrain has its own exotic type of gaucho as well. Here, the gauchos raise sheep, not cattle, and even more surprisingly, many speak English. The English language is spoken here because many of the ancestors of the Patagonian gauchos were **immigrants**[10] from Scotland. Several of these settlers came to the area during the 19th century, including the ancestors of Eduardo Halliday and his father, Jimmy. These two gauchos run a ranch in Patagonia, and for them, this strange terrain seems like the perfect place to live.

---

[8]**glacier:** a large mass of ice
[9]**exotic:** unusual and attractive; especially things from other countries
[10]**immigrant:** a person who moves to another country to live

The Hallidays enjoy living in the region for a number of reasons, but Jimmy has a specific reason for liking it. He explains that the most refreshing aspect about living in Patagonia is that there is space everywhere around their ranch. This enables him to see a long way in all directions, which is a very different experience from living in a town or city. The land is also rich, he says, and produces everything that he and his family need to live. Life on the plains of Patagonia is difficult, even harsh, but over the years the gauchos here have learned how to adjust and succeed.

Eduardo has lived his entire life on the family ranch and has learned the traditional ways from his father. The goal of every gaucho is self-reliance, and these gauchos of Patagonia are no different. Because the ranch is so remote, father and son have to utilize everything they have available. This also means they don't abandon anything quickly and often use and reuse everything they have, including their bags and their boots. After all, it's a long way to go to buy new ones.

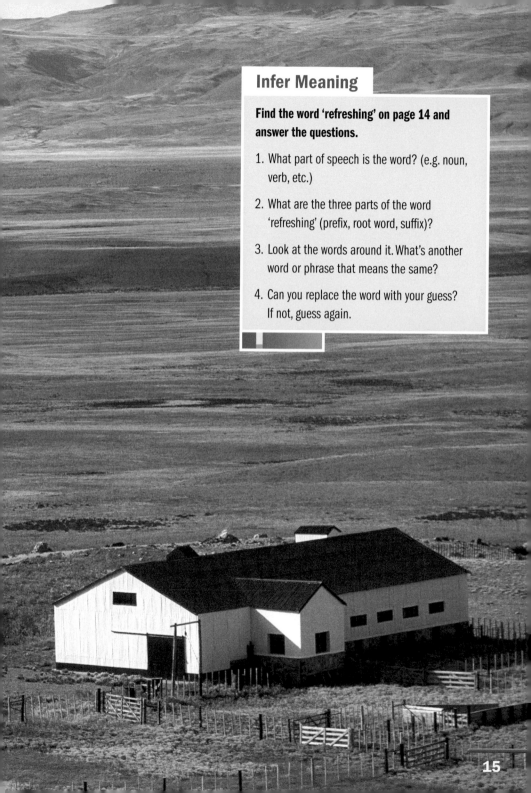

Infer Meaning

Find the word 'refreshing' on page 14 and answer the questions.

1. What part of speech is the word? (e.g. noun, verb, etc.)

2. What are the three parts of the word 'refreshing' (prefix, root word, suffix)?

3. Look at the words around it. What's another word or phrase that means the same?

4. Can you replace the word with your guess? If not, guess again.

Gaucho sometimes use boleadoras to catch rheas.

In addition to maintaining their self-reliance, gauchos also focus on maintaining tradition. Patagonia is a land that was once thought to be too harsh to support life. But being a gaucho here—and everywhere—means **adapting**[11] to the landscape while holding on to tradition. Gauchos are experts at adjusting to their surroundings. Here in Patagonia, for example, they use the *boleadora*, a kind of **weapon**[12] which was acquired from the local native people. The *boleadora* is made of leather and small stones, and it is far from easy to use. Both Eduardo and his father are able to use the weapon though, and Eduardo is now teaching his son how to use one. By doing so, he's helping to sustain the family traditions.

Out in the countryside, the gauchos still use *boleadoras* to catch small animals, such as the *rhea*, a type of South American bird which does not fly. Pursuing the animals on their fast horses is no problem for the talented gauchos, whereas hitting the animals while riding can be extremely difficult. As the gauchos fly like the wind along the plains on their strong horses, the *rheas* run swiftly ahead of them. As they run, the small birds constantly cut tight turns to the left and right in order to avoid being caught. It's an exciting chase for both horse and rider, but in the end, the *rheas* manage to get away—this time.

---

[11]**adapt:** change to function in a new way; adjust or modify
[12]**weapon:** a tool used to harm or kill

Twenty-nine hundred kilometers away to the north of Patagonia is the region of Salta. Here the stony hills and rough terrain have produced yet a different kind of gaucho, one who has been able to survive and even succeed in this harsh place. The gauchos here were once fierce soldiers for Argentina, and they won recognition and respect in the Argentine War of Independence from Spain. They are famous for their huge leather chaps and their red ponchos, and the Salta gauchos celebrate their proud traditions in an annual parade. During the parade, they walk through the streets on their strong horses and display their fine clothing and horsemanship skills, but these gauchos are capable of much more than just riding in parades.

Like all gauchos, the gauchos of Salta rely on their horses for both work and play. They also often train smaller work horses for use on the ranches as well as bigger horses for use in shows. One of the best horsemen in the area is **Rudecindo Campos**.[13] Rudecindo loves being a gaucho and says that it's the life he's always wanted. He explains in his own words, "In life there are all kinds of people: engineers, doctors, and gauchos. I knew I had to choose one or the other. I have always had a gaucho soul and I like being a gaucho."

However, choosing the life of a gaucho means more than just working with horses. Just as it is in Corrientes, a strict code of ethics and principles is essential to the gaucho lifestyle in Salta as well. Rudecindo's father Don Coco Campos explains that here, too, being a gaucho means being good and kind, and not rejecting requests for help. "It's not only knowing how to catch an animal with a rope, use a saddle, or ride a horse. It's also about being good and kind. When you ask a gaucho a favor," he says, "he must not refuse. He does it."

---

[13]**Rudecindo Campos:** [rʊdəsɪntoʊ kæmpoʊs]

While the gaucho code of kindness and respect is admirable, ethics don't feed a family. At times, it is difficult to make enough money while working as a gaucho. In order for his family to survive, Rudecindo must work at a part-time job just so that he can continue doing what he does best—training horses. Rudecindo specializes in training a strong little type of horse that comes from this area called a criollo. The criollo is one of the few animals that can round up cattle in this rough terrain which is covered with **thorns**.[14] To protect themselves from the environment, horse and rider rely on a special type of leather chaps. The thick leather of the chaps protects the pair from injuries as they round up the last of the cattle and bring them back to the ranch. The horses, too, are specially trained to race along independently, so the riders rarely need to use the reins. This allows the gaucho to focus more intently on following the cattle instead of watching the dangers of the path.

---

[14]**thorn:** sharp, pointed parts of some plants

Identify Cause and Effect

1. What is the main cause for Rudecindo needing to get a part-time job?

2. What two effects has the rough terrain of Salta had on gauchos and their horses?

In Salta, each time the gauchos successfully return all of the cattle safely back to the ranch, there is traditionally a lively fiesta. The fiesta is a small party for all of the people who have taken part in the event. As they dance and sing at the fiesta, it's easy to see the important role that women play in the lives of the gauchos. Rudecindo's wife, who comes from the city originally, talks about being a gaucho's wife. "It's very difficult to adapt to the slower pace of the *campo*," she says. "In the city, you live faster and you are less attentive to nature. We've lost that in the city. We've lost some of our humanity, which my husband hasn't lost. He's not caught up in the **trivia**[15] of everyday life. You can really get consumed by small things, and you forget what's important."

So does living in the *campo* really make a person more human? Does it make one pay special attention to what's really important in life? Rudecindo seems to feel that way. "If I go into town for two weeks," he explains, "I can't wait to get home to the horses, to the smell of the countryside, and the wet earth after a rain." He concludes, "I love this life." As in all regions of the country, here too there seems to be a special relationship between the gaucho and the countryside—and a great love of being a gaucho.

---

[15]**trivia:** unimportant things

In the end, the story of today's gaucho in Argentina may be one of adaptation. Over the years, the gauchos have adapted to climate, to landscape, and to traditional ways of life that sustain them. Don José Ansola may have one of the best perspectives. "For Argentina," he says, "it's very important for people to treasure this proud and **honorable legacy**.[16] We must be sure that whatever else happens to us, we never lose our heritage, our gaucho way of life." Don José is not alone in his dream. The proud and self-reliant gauchos of Corrientes, Patagonia, and Salta are all helping to retain the traditional lifestyle of the gauchos forever.

---

[16]**honorable legacy:** something that is well-respected and passed on or left by an earlier generation

After You Read

1. On page 4, the word 'scarcely' can be replaced by:
    A. potentially
    B. hardly
    C. typically
    D. unlikely

2. Which of the following is NOT a part of the gaucho lifestyle?
    A. horses
    B. solitude
    C. treasure
    D. *mate*

3. Why are wild horses broken?
    A. so gauchos can show cruelty
    B. because there are too many
    C. because gauchos love them
    D. so that a person can ride them

4. An appropriate heading for page 10 is:
    A. Nation Respects Gaucho Tradition
    B. Gauchos Living in Antarctica
    C. Argentina Needs More Gauchos
    D. Lonely Gauchos in Patagonia

5. Unlike the gauchos in Corrientes, the gauchos in Patagonia:
    A. speak French
    B. raise sheep
    C. have families
    D. like cold weather

6. What is the purpose of paragraph 2 on page 14?
    A. to introduce information about the climate of Patagonia
    B. to explain that Eduardo is tired of the life on the ranch
    C. to demonstrate a conflict between the father and son
    D. to illustrate how gauchos can remain self-reliant

7. In paragraph 1 on page 17, to whom does 'they' refer?
   A. gauchos in Patagonia
   B. *boleadoras*
   C. native people
   D. Eduardo and his father

8. The gauchos of the Salta region wear _____ ponchos.
   A. huge
   B. leather
   C. red
   D. heavy

9. What is the main purpose of Rudecindo's father's comments in paragraph 2 on page 21?
   A. to show that Rudecindo has a gaucho soul
   B. to give an example of the gaucho code of ethics
   C. to express regret that his son became a gaucho
   D. to talk about the importance of gauchos in Argentina

10. On page 22, the word 'intently' describes doing something with:
    A. skill
    B. admiration
    C. justification
    D. focus

11. The writer would probably characterize Rudecindo's wife as:
    A. relevant
    B. annoying
    C. domestic
    D. insecure

12. Which of the following is accurate about gauchos all over Argentina?
    A. They are concerned about maintaining their traditions.
    B. They are satisfied with their lives.
    C. They are upset that tourists don't visit the countryside.
    D. They are thankful that their families are with them.

Dear Lee, April 3rd

How are things back home? Things here are great! We've only been in Argentina for a few days, but we've already had so many remarkable experiences! We arrived in Buenos Aires last Saturday and spent a couple of days just exploring this fascinating city. The first evening we visited Puerto Madero. Prior to this visit, it was a rather unattractive neighborhood, but there's been an astonishing transformation in the past ten years. It's now full of wonderful places to eat. We had a delicious dinner in an outdoor cafe and relaxed for hours just watching people walk by.

The next morning we visited several of the famous squares in downtown Buenos Aires. To me the most striking one was the three-block-long Plaza del Congreso. They say the whole thing was constructed in less than a year, which I find to be an unbelievable achievement! We also visited the residence of the president, the nearby Casa Rosada, which means 'pink house' in English. The most interesting thing about the city for me is the people; everyone is absolutely beautiful—both men and women. They could all be movie stars! It must be something special about the lifestyle here.

On Tuesday we decided to visit the gaucho museum in San Antonio de Areco. However, on our way there, we were lucky enough to come across a traditional Argentinean gaucho event—complete with a horse show. We stopped to take advantage of the opportunity to see Argentinean gauchos in action. They did some really amazing things that showed off their excellent riding skills. I have to admit, I was cheering as loudly as the next person.

Iguazu Falls

Later in the week we flew to Iguazu National Park to see the waterfalls. The falls were incredibly impressive, but what I enjoyed most was a side trip we took. Our guide led us down a three-kilometer path deep into rain forest terrain. It was the loveliest, most exotic and peaceful place I've ever seen. It really felt like I was in another world. Here's a picture so you can see how wonderful it is—I'll send more pictures and info later when I update my journal!

See you soon!
Marco

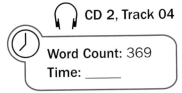

CD 2, Track 04

Word Count: 369
Time: _____

Vocabulary List

adapt (17, 25, 27)
cattle (3, 10, 13, 22, 25)
chaps (3, 18, 22)
ethics (10, 21, 22)
exotic (13)
gaucho (2, 3, 4, 6, 9, 10, 13, 14, 16, 17, 18, 21, 22, 23, 25, 27)
glacier (13)
harsh (9, 13, 14, 17, 18)
heritage (2, 27)
honorable legacy (27)
hospitality (10)
immigrant (13)
mate (6)
pampas (2, 4)
poncho (3, 18)
put up with (9)
ranch (3, 7, 9, 13, 14, 21, 22, 25)
reins (3, 22)
remote (2, 6, 13, 14)
saddle (3, 21)
self-reliant (2, 4, 14, 17, 27)
solitude (6, 7, 10)
terrain (2, 4, 13, 18, 22, 23)
thorn (22)
trivia (25)
weapon (17)

Metric Conversion Chart

Area
1 hectare = 2.471 acres

Length
1 centimeter = .394 inches
1 meter = 1.094 yards
1 kilometer = .621 miles

Temperature
0° Celsius = 32° Fahrenheit

Volume
1 liter = 1.057 quarts

Weight
1 gram = .035 ounces
1 kilogram = 2.2 pounds